DOGS SET VIII

PORTUGUESE WATER DOGS

Jill C. Wheeler
ABDO Publishing Company

visit us at
www.abdopublishing.com

Published by ABDO Publishing Company, 8000 West 78th Street, Edina, Minnesota 55439. Copyright © 2010 by Abdo Consulting Group, Inc. International copyrights reserved in all countries. No part of this book may be reproduced in any form without written permission from the publisher. The Checkerboard Library™ is a trademark and logo of ABDO Publishing Company.

Printed in the United States of America, North Mankato, Minnesota.
082009
012010

 PRINTED ON RECYCLED PAPER

Cover Photo: Alamy
Interior Photos: Alamy pp. 7, 11, 15, 19; AP Images pp. 5, 9, 13; Corbis pp. 10, 17; iStockphoto p. 21

Series Coordinator: Tamara L. Britton
Editors: Tamara L. Britton, Heidi M.D. Elston
Art Direction: Jaime Martens

Library of Congress Cataloging-in-Publication Data

Wheeler, Jill C., 1964-
  Portuguese water dogs / Jill C. Wheeler.
       p. cm. -- (Dogs)
  Includes index.
  ISBN 978-1-60453-784-0
  1. Portuguese water dog--Juvenile literature. I. Title.
  SF429.P87W44 2010
  636.73--dc22
                          2009027579

CONTENTS

THE DOG FAMILY

Dogs are among the world's most popular pets. Worldwide, there are nearly 400 different **breeds**! All these dogs are members of the **Canidae** family. This name comes from the Latin word for "dog," which is *canis*. Wolves, coyotes, and foxes are part of this family, too.

For thousands of years, humans relied on dogs to help them hunt. They also used dogs to guard their families and belongings.

Eventually, people developed different breeds to perform specific tasks. Portuguese water dogs were bred to work on fishing boats. These excellent swimmers helped fishermen catch fish.

In 2009, U.S. president Baraok Obama and his family welcomed Bo, a Portuguese water dog puppy.

PORTUGUESE WATER DOGS

It is believed that the Portuguese water dog's ancestors came from the border area between Russia and China. These ancient dogs herded cattle, sheep, camels, and horses.

Nomadic warriors captured some of these dogs. They took them south to Spain and Portugal. These dogs would develop into Portuguese water dogs.

In time, Portuguese fishermen trained the dogs. They learned to herd fish into nets and retrieve lost fishing gear. The dogs also carried messages between boats at sea. On shore, they guarded the boats and the daily catch.

The Portuguese water dog came to the United States in 1958. In 1983, the **American Kennel Club (AKC)** recognized the **breed**. Today, this working dog is a popular family companion.

Worldwide, there are about 10,000 registered Portuguese water dogs.

What They're Like

Portuguese water dogs are intelligent, loyal, obedient, and hardworking. They are strong enough to swim all day, and they are excellent divers. The dogs have webbed feet, with skin between their toes. This helps them swim fast!

Portuguese water dogs are in the working dog group. Working dogs are used to herd livestock and retrieve objects. They are happiest when they can do these things with their owners.

These energetic and social animals love to be with their families. They do not do well when left alone for long periods of time. They have even been known to follow their owners around the house!

President Obama and his daughter Malia walk Bo.

COAT AND COLOR

Portuguese water dogs have a naturally **waterproof** coat. It can be either curly or wavy. The dogs are single coated. This means they do not have an undercoat that sheds.

The lion clip

Portuguese water dogs still shed a little. However, they shed much less than many other **breeds**. Because of this, they are considered to be **hypoallergenic**.

These dogs need frequent brushing and an occasional

haircut. The **AKC** accepts two haircuts, or clips.
The lion clip features longer hair in the front. Hair
along the middle, hindquarters, and **muzzle** is
closely clipped. For the
working-retriever clip, all
hair is trimmed
to one inch (2.5 cm) long.

   Coat colors can be solid
black, brown, or white. Or,
they can combine black or
brown with white.
Many Portuguese water
dogs with combination
coats have a patch of white
on their chests.

The working-retriever clip

SIZE

Portuguese water dogs are medium-sized dogs. Males usually weigh 42 to 60 pounds (19 to 27 kg). Females generally weigh between 35 and 50 pounds (16 and 22 kg).

Males stand between 20 and 23 inches (51 and 58 cm) tall. A height of 22 inches (56 cm) is considered ideal for male show dogs. Females stand 17 to 21 inches (43 to 53 cm) tall. The ideal height for female show dogs is 19 inches (48 cm).

Portuguese water dogs are slightly longer than they are tall. Their heads are large with a broad forehead. These dogs have powerful legs and a thick tail. They use the tail as a **rudder** when swimming!

U.S. senator Edward M. Kennedy walks with Splash, his Portuguese water dog.

CARE

All dogs need exercise, and Portuguese water dogs are no exception! They need a lot of vigorous exercise. They especially enjoy swimming and playing in water.

It is important to check a dog's eyes, nose, mouth, skin, and feet for problems. A good time to do this is when grooming the coat. A dog's teeth should be brushed daily. Its nails should be trimmed regularly, too.

Portuguese water dogs can develop health conditions. These include problems with joints and eyesight. A veterinarian can help keep a Portuguese water dog healthy and happy. The veterinarian can also **spay** or **neuter** the dog. And, he or she can provide regular checkups and **vaccines**.

In Portugal, the breed is called Cão de Agua (kown d'ahgwa). This means "Dog of Water" in the Portuguese language.

FEEDING

Dog owners must make sure their pets have fresh water and food every day. Select a good quality food for your dog.

Some owners feed their pets commercial food. It comes in dry, moist, and semimoist varieties. Others like to feed their dogs natural diets, such as raw meat or fish.

Whatever the diet, each Portuguese water dog needs a different amount of food. How much to feed a dog depends on its age, size, and activity level.

Puppies need several small meals every day. Older dogs can eat one larger meal each day. A veterinarian can suggest an appropriate diet based on a dog's needs.

President Obama and Bo play in the White House. Bo was a gift to the president's family from Senator Edward M. Kennedy.

THINGS THEY NEED

Portuguese water dogs require lots of activity and attention. They need both physical and mental exercise. Portuguese water dog owners must be willing to spend lots of time with their dogs. If the dogs are left alone, they can get into trouble!

Of course, Portuguese water dogs also like water. They love to swim and dive. Walks and runs along a beach are ideal activities for this **breed**.

Portuguese water dogs like to be outside. So, they will need a collar with a license and tags. Toys help keep these active dogs busy. A bed provides a soft, warm place to rest.

A loving family, socialization, and training will result in a happy, well-behaved pet.

PUPPIES

Portuguese water dogs give birth about 63 days after mating. They have an average of six puppies in a **litter**. The puppies need to stay with their mother until they are 8 to 12 weeks old. Then, they can move with their new family to a forever home.

If a Portuguese water dog is right for your family, look for a reputable **breeder**. Look for playful and curious puppies. They should be willing to approach people and be held.

When your puppy comes home, make an appointment to see the veterinarian. Be sure to feed your new puppy the same diet it ate at the breeder's. Then, slowly begin to feed it the diet suggested by the veterinarian.

Introduce your new puppy to different experiences, animals, and people right away. **Socialization** and training will help it grow into a well-adjusted dog. A healthy Portuguese water dog will be a loving family member for about 12 years.

A puppy needs time to adjust to a new home. Show the puppy its bed, food, and water. Then, let it explore!

GLOSSARY

American Kennel Club (AKC) - an organization that studies and promotes interest in purebred dogs.

breed - a group of animals sharing the same ancestors and appearance. A breeder is a person who raises animals. Raising animals is often called breeding them.

Canidae (KAN-uh-dee) - the scientific Latin name for the dog family. Members of this family are called canids. They include domestic dogs, wolves, jackals, foxes, and coyotes.

hypoallergenic - unlikely to cause an allergic reaction.

litter - all of the puppies born at one time to a mother dog.

muzzle - an animal's nose and jaws.

neuter (NOO-tuhr) - to remove a male animal's reproductive organs.

nomadic - relating to a member of a tribe that moves from place to place.

rudder - a blade on the bottom of a boat near the back. When moved, it causes the boat to turn.

socialize - to accustom an animal or a person to spending time with others.

spay - to remove a female animal's reproductive organs.

vaccine (vak-SEEN) - a shot given to animals or humans to prevent them from getting an illness or a disease.

waterproof - not allowing water to pass through.

WEB SITES

To learn more about Portuguese water dogs, visit ABDO Publishing Company on the World Wide Web at **www.abdopublishing.com**. Web sites about Portuguese water dogs are featured on our Book Links page. These links are routinely monitored and updated to provide the most current information available.

INDEX